We Are Our Own Lions

poetry and prose by
Damien Stednitz

an egoboy studios production

I0182434

We Are Our Own Lions
Copyright © 2006 by Damien Stednitz

All photos © Jayme Stednitz
Published by Egoboy Studios   Sunland, CA

All rights reserved. No part of this book may be used or
reproduced in any manner whatsoever without written permission,
except in the case of brief quotations embodied in critical articles
and reviews. Printed in the United States of America.

This book is a work of fiction. Names, characters, places and
incidents are products of the author's imagination or are used
fictitiously. Any resemblance to actual events or locales or
persons, living or dead is entirely coincidental.

To contact the author please send an email to
damien.stednitz@hotmail.com.

"Jerry Springer" first appeared in True Poet Magazine.
"Degas" first appeared in The Flintlock (NWU literary journal).
"Parental Guidance Strongly Suggested" first appeared in
Speechless Magazine.

Second Edition   March 2011

ISBN: 978-0-6154676-6-5 $10.00

This book is dedicated to my parents, Don & Patsy and my siblings: Dustin, Seth, Tessie and Sarah. I come from a good pride.

&

To Jayme, always.

Table of Contents

Jerry Springer

Jerry, you were it
when I was in college
Jayme and I
watched faithfully
continually dumbfounded by
the daily trailer truths
you uncovered

we watched
jaw-dropped
every Tuesday / Thursday
between
Mass Comm and
Sociology of the Family

we debated Steve's max
bench press and we
marveled at your
continual shock
your always sincere
surprise
as breasts were bared
chairs were thrown
paternities were revealed
all to the repetitious
cheering of your
name

for one hour each week

Oprah was ashamed
Chicago was Rome
Studio 12 was the Coliseum
and we were our own lions
feeding on each other

I don't watch anymore Jerry

I'd love to say
it's because I'm more
mature now and no longer
subscribe to your low brand
of entertainment

but Jerry
the truth is
I don't watch anymore
because

my jaw won't drop

I'm no longer shocked
by the violence and betrayals
the degradation and humiliation
I've seen it all too many times before
and it makes me feel

nothing

and Jerry, I know you
want us to take care of ourselves
and each other, but Jerry
I think you left us hollow

my final thought for
today's show
is that my generation may now
be dead inside
numb
barren
lions gnawing on bone

Degas

The elevator hummed and my stomach alerted me to movement that my eyes couldn't detect. The box pulled me upwards and I had that familiar nagging in the back of my mind as to whether or not I could trust Dan Dolan. Dan's signature graced the yellowed paper framed at eye level which certified the safety of the device I was in. When I heard the ding of survival I quietly thanked Dan and God for doing their respective jobs in getting me to the 7th floor safely. The doors to freedom opened and I stepped out, happy to be on more trustworthy ground.

Clean. Everything there was clean: the neutral carpet, the nurses that walked meaningfully about, the doctors who drank vital coffee and picked up charts with sacred hands. It was all immaculate. The dirt in my flower pot felt as out of place there as I did. I felt awkward for lacking an illness or a doctorate. I walked carefully down the hall simultaneously trying to not spill dirt or bump into anything or anyone of dire importance.

713. The black room numbers gleamed next to the open door with an impossible shine. The room was overly crowded with furniture and dorm room small. I felt almost in my element. My mother lay flat on a crooked bed, asleep. She was coming home from her short stay in this sanitary solitude soon. Unfortunately, break was over before her hospital stay was. This was the inevitable conflict of university scheduling and a bursting appendix. I sat the dirt and plant on her table both carefully and quietly. She still woke up and for a fleeting moment, out of habit, I felt the familiar fear of being caught sneaking in past curfew.

She looked weak and tired, but happy to see me. We talked for half an hour and agreed that we were both doing fine, the Oscars weren't going to be that interesting this year, that my girlfriend was too shy, and that it was really about time for me to get going. I said the usual goodbye and promise to call, and then I walked out of room 713.

As I turned down the hallway to leave Edgar Degas stopped me and held me right where I stood. His painting *Melancholy* clung perfectly to the wall above and to the right of a contrasting sign which read: CANCER WARD LEFT.

The painted woman stared at the sign with her painted, half-closed eyes from beneath her cleansed glass frame. She demanded my attention like only beauty can. She owned my eyes and mind then as she had countless times before from her page in my worn art book.

A distant voice uttered a profound understatement, "Nice painting."

"Yeah, I love Degas. I got a book of his work back at school," I answered distracted, still enraptured by the painting.

I finally broke my gaze and faced a brutal scar. I inadvertently stepped backwards as my eyes frantically tried to make sense out of what they perceived.

A boy. A sick boy. A sick boy with half his head shaved and a huge, vicious "C" where doctors had entered like God and left like man. He leaned heavily on an aluminum walker. He wasn't more than thirteen.

"Sorry," his words were slow, a little forced, "I didn't mean to freak you out."

My eyes stared at the sad scar.

"I told them to shave the other side too. Then at least I could have had cancer and a mohawk."

The frail boy smiled at me. It wasn't until I saw the whiteness of his teeth that I realized he had made a joke.

"Yeah," my mouth replied, not knowing what to say.

"I like her," the sick boy said of Edgar and mine's lady, "she's dealing with a lot. You can tell by the look on her face. There's pain in her face, but she's still beautiful, you know?"

I looked at the beautiful boy and nodded, but I didn't know what he meant. Not really, I didn't know like he knew.

I awkwardly excused myself from the overwhelming beauty and pain. My legs took me towards the elevator quickly. I watched the boy as the elevator doors hissed close. He was leaning heavily on his fake legs, staring at the painting, repeating it. The identical portraits burned in my mind.

Images of dirt, Degas, defiant smiles and sewn flesh stayed with me as I rushed to my car. Once the car door closed, sealing me in silence, I wept.

The Car, the Thimble, the Dog and the Guy on the Horse

PLAY.

Blockbuster Video owns North America. They are larger than their next 500 competitors combined. I know this because there used to be a little yellow sticker on the checkout counter at Blockbuster that told you this. It let you know that you were renting with the winning team. They don't have those stickers up anymore. I think it has to do with the American underdog thing. There's just too many of us who have been chosen last in gym class, too many of us harassed by bullies.

REWIND.

Mark Fresher, that was his name. A big, kind of chubby kid who when he was younger got tortured by his older brothers who were still trying to deal with their parents' divorce. Mark kept all of his sibling anger inside and unleashed it in little spurts on unsuspecting kids. Kids like me.

He chased me home from school every day for months when I was in 2nd grade. He would repeat various phrases he had gathered from television and movies that he felt were insults.

"I'll kill you, you Jew baby!" he would yell. I'm Catholic and have been all my life; of course, Mark knew this because we went to the same church.

"You better run, you womanizer or I'll kill you!"

Womanizer, that was his favorite. My guess is it was something he heard his mom call his dad after the divorce. I'm sure in Mark's mind it was the worse thing someone could be.

My world was fear as the clock ticked towards 3:00. My only saving grace was about once a week Mark would get in trouble during class and would have to stay after school. But, more often than not, it was a mad chase to see whether I could get to my front yard before Mark got to me. I wasn't a very fast kid.

Knowing that sheer speed wasn't going to grant me salvation, I tried other solutions. I watched *The Karate Kid* with a passion that had my parents worried. I dreamed of the day when Mark would catch up with me and I would turn, arms raised up like wings flapping, stand on one leg and give him the kick that would break his jaw. It never happened.

What I did start doing was cutting through an alley on the way home. For three glorious days in a row I made it home unscathed. It was so stealthy of me. I felt like a secret agent or a ninja. Mark eventually figured out my secret route. The main problem with alleys is that they supply bullies with trash cans to throw at you.

That's how I got the scar on my knee. I was running for my life as angry trash can lids flew over my head like UFO's. To compound the situation Jimmy Broward's cat Felix ran out in front of me as I dodged Mark's trash onslaught. Instead of stepping on Felix I opted to slide skidding into the scared tabby like he was home plate. My leg tore open on broken glass, Felix hissed and scampered off. Mark seeing that I had actually injured myself ran away faster than I ever had during one of our pursuits.

I limped home blubbering, thinking of band-aids and ice cream. I got both within five minutes of walking through my front door. It was that day, bowl of butter pecan in front of me, tears mixing with the melting goodness, that I broke one of the unspoken rules of childhood: I told on the bully. I gave Mark up to my parents. Now, my ultimate fear was that my mom would call Mark's mom and then Mark would make me pay for it later. That's not what happened.

I'll never forget the look of fear on Mark's face as my dad held Mark two feet up in the air, pinned to the oak tree in our front yard. I had a true feeling of satisfaction as my father's booming grown-up baritone informed Mark that he wouldn't live to see 13. Mark never bugged me again and I think I always held my dad in a little bit higher regard from then on. Unfortunately, I don't still live with my parents.

FAST FORWARD. PLAY.

Blockbuster sent me a letter today. Apparently, they're going to notify a collection agency if I don't pay them the $2.12 late fee I owe them for a movie I rented there two months ago. It was a Steve Martin movie, not really all that funny. It was one of his post-"The Jerk" and pre-"Roxanne" films. Now I had put it in their little drop box thing the night it was due. But, apparently even though they're open until midnight, movies dropped into the drop box at 11:15 are considered late.

Further, since there is a buster on every block I just haven't gone back to that location to give them their money. So now they're going to send guys in suits after me for an amount of money that wouldn't even wash and dry an entire load of laundry at the laundromat. This is where I was when I opened the letter from the Big Yellow and Blue.

(By the way, washing clothes is a complete mystery to me, I'm never sure what I'm supposed to do with those Snuggle bear sheets.) So anyways, here I am with a load of my t-shirts all turning a lovely hue of pink and now I have to go pay Blockbuster an amount of money I probably have in the cup holder of my car.

Upon the drying of said pink shirts I drive over and walk into the sensory overload that is Blockbuster Video. The monitors above my head blare what's happening on the Blockbuster Channel (yes, their own channel). The woman from the hand lotion commercials is telling me the social merit of the collective works of Keanu Reeves. (Did you know his name means cool breeze over mountains?) Continually I hear the mantra that I should make my night a Blockbuster night...it's a near Orwellian chant.

I try to focus and approach the counter. The girl behind it running the computer (her name was Kim) is kind of cute. Under normal circumstances I would have quickly grabbed a Meg Ryan film off the shelf. Thus, I could begin to flirt with her a little bit while renting a movie that shows her what a sensitive guy I am: "Sleepless? Oh I loved that one too!"

This actually does work; the only problem with dating video store employees is that they never want to go see any movies because they are forced to deal with them all the time.

Now since I work at a restaurant and hate to eat out that pretty much eliminates the old dinner / movie standby. Unfortunately, you can't base a relationship for very long on just sex and miniature golf.

I leave Meg on the shelf tonight though, because this isn't normal circumstances. I'm pissed off. I'm pissed off that a multi-million dollar corporation that has manifest destiny in the video rental market is harassing me for two bucks. At least when Mark picked on me I could chalk it up to the fact that he was psycho, what's Blockbuster's excuse?

I ask Kim politely enough to get me the manager. After a moment Dave comes over from overpricing the previously viewed movie section. His smile is as plastic as the videos he panders.

"How may I help you tonight, sir?"

"Well, Dave. I'd like to know why you guys are threatening me with a collection agency over $2.12."

"Oh," a look of near sincere concern, "did you have an extended viewing fee?"

PAUSE.

Extended viewing fee. God, I love that. They'll charge me for being late, but they won't actually call it "late". Instead they make it sound like I just liked the movie so much I wanted to "extend" my viewing. Please.

PLAY.

"Dave, if you care so much about my feelings that you won't call it a late fee why don't you just write off the $2 I owe? Then my feelings would definitely be taken care of."

Dave's smile melts like a VHS tape on the dashboard in June.

"Sir, in your membership agreement you agreed to pay all applicable fees that come with the privilege of renting videos here. Now, when you incur an extended viewing fee we just expect the courtesy of you paying it promptly. If that's not done we find it productive to remind you. It's nothing personal."

"Shit, Dave if you're so big into reminding me why didn't you call me up when you saw the movie was going to be late? If you're that concerned why not give me a ring? I know you got my phone number. Why not give me a ring and ask if I realized I was extending my viewing of your video? Do you have any scissors?"

I chop up my membership card as a line of people wanting to get home with their new Jean-Claude Van Damme film bitch behind me. I throw the scraps in Dave's face and tell him to go to hell. I feel pretty cool up until the point that I try to exit through the entrance. Since there's no handle from the inside, I have to turn around and walk through all the shocked renters, pass through the sensors guaranteeing that I'm not stealing videos and then finally I make it out into the dark, movieless night.

HEAD CLEANER.

I'm out of the loop. It's been two weeks of Blockbuster exile now. The grocery stores I try to rent from never have the new releases I want. It's hard to drive down the streets at night. Every corner I stop at the blue and yellow glow at me, mocking me. A person paid me last night for their meal with a Blockbuster Visa card. They're everywhere and now I'm left out. The girl I'm seeing always wants to come back to my place and watch movies. I think that's what's going to make me break down. I'm going to go back, I can feel it already. There's no other place to go. They own it all, and if they piss me off, it doesn't matter. They know I'll come back. They got all the movies and I got nothing but an empty VCR starving for food.

The Man in the Red Suit

I'm writing this in the hopes that once I finish it I will read it and think it all sounds idiotic. That I can merely dismiss it as me being paranoid or overly imaginative, hell I'd even settle for delusional at this point. It all happened at Circuit City when I was doing my weekly DVD hunt on an extended lunch break.

I was chatting it up with one of the clerks about how cool the new *Transformers* box set is, when my day took somewhat of an odd turn. A small Asian girl in a massive Spongebob coat walked up to me and said, "You're Jake Colloway."

This, in of itself, may seem like an inconsequential item not worthy of nervously typing up a few pages. However there are three key things to take into consideration: one, my name is Jake Calloway. Two, unlike my friend Rob The Clerk; I don't make a habit of wearing a name tag. Three, I've never seen this girl before.

"You're Jake, aren't you? You're Jake," she said and smiled a toothy grin exactly like the one ole Mr. Squarepants was giving me from her hood.

I looked casually around the store for a mom, but none were to be seen. I did make a mental note of a blonde picking up a Ben Harper CD. Hot and good taste in music, a win-win.

"Jake, Jake, Jake" the girl whispered three times, "Jake Calloway."

I immediately looked at my suit thinking for some reason maybe today I was wearing a name tag. Other than some cat hair from Mr. T (my cat has an unexplainable mowhawk) my suit was free of any distinguishing signs. It was just a plain grey suit.

"Jake Calloway, that's who you are."

Rob The Clerk began to look somewhat concerned at the look of confusion on my face. I activated my mental Rolodex and tried to find where this girl belonged. She was too young to be the girl that sold me Girl Scout cookies, none of my friends have kids, and she wasn't the child of anyone I worked with.

"Do I know you?" I asked trying to sound calm, cheerful and grown up.

"Has he found you?" She asked never stopping with her toothy grin. She was missing a tooth up front. Her eyes were nearly black.

"Is someone looking for me? Does your Daddy know me?" I asked, hoping my pants wouldn't rip as I squatted down to be at eye level with my new found friend. At the Daddy question she giggled.

"My Daddy doesn't know you silly!"

"Does your Mommy?"

"No, Jake, you're funny."

It was time for the 25,000 dollar question.

"Then how do you know my name?"

At this I got more toothy Spongebob grin and was reminded why I don't talk to six-year-olds on a regular basis: they're not the most rationale conversationalists around.

"You're Jake," she said as if I was an American Idol finalist that everyone knew. I'm not.

"You're right, I'm Jake. What's your name?"

"I'm Sonja" she grinned and actually stuck out her hand as if we were business associates. If anything she had good manners.

"Sonja, can you show me who's looking for me so I can talk to them?"

Her brow furrowed and she leaned in close, whispering, "The man in the red suit is looking for you, Jake."

At this I began scanning the room for some sort of Circuit City manager in some new, important red Circuit City uniform/suit. Maybe I had been selected to get some distinguished customer award. Seeing no one I turned back to my enigma of the day.

"Can you show me where this man is?"

Another giggle now, "He's not here silly! He's never here. He's in The Other Place."

The weird emphasis she used on "The Other Place" made me feel that she wasn't meaning Best Buy. I was just about to ask the bonus round question of where the hell this "Other Place" was when Mom showed up.

"Sonja! Who are you talking to?" Mom rushed over looking somewhat concerned. I was glad my good bud Rob had witnessed everything in case the kid launched into a story of how I was trying to give her candy and get her into my car.

I extended my hand and put on a sales smile, "I'm..."

"That's Jake Calloway; the man in the red suit is looking for him."

At this Mom looked almost through me and all she could utter was a worried "oh." Her eyes were as big as the flat screen TV's in back. I wasn't really sure how to proceed. My hand still was out there awaiting a shake. Mom regarded it like I was trying to hand her anthrax. I tried to salvage.

"I'm sorry ma'am do I know you two? My apologies I seem to have forgotten where we met."

"No, no you don't know us." She muttered lost in other thoughts, her eyes no longer looking at me. She was scanning the room for an exit. "I'm sorry if Sonja bothered you. We have to go."

"Mommy!" Sonja yelled, digging in. "The man in the red suit is looking for him, his name is Jake Calloway! He has a cat with funny hair!"

This was right about the point my "what the hell?" meter hit its all time high. Mom had already thrown down the printer cartridge she was going to buy and was rushing for the door with Sonja Squarepants in tow.

"Excuse me, ma'am?" I started after them leaving my friend Rob behind. I was trying hard to keep my voice at a non-scene making level. I caught back up with them right at the automatic doors.

"I'm sorry ma'am I don't mean to bother you, but how does she know these things about me. Do I know you from somewhere?"

"His cat's name is Mr. T, he's gray," the little girl spouted. She was a fount of information about me.

"Honey stop it! What have I told you about this?" Mom snapped, for a moment I thought she may hit the girl.

"No, she's right. That is my cat's name and he does have funny hair. How does she know that?"

"Sir, we have to go, I'm sorry…I'm sorry for you."

With that she headed out of the store, dragging the girl behind her. I followed like a confused puppy uttering an occasional "ma'am" or "please, ma'am wait". People walking into the store were staring.

"Bye Jake!" Sonja waved with the arm that her mother wasn't trying to pull out of socket, "Tell the man in the red suit..."

She was then shut into a Montero which tore out of the parking lot like a monkey on meth was driving it.

This all happened a week ago. I've spent the last few days trying to figure out if I've ever met Sonja and her mom before. I'm really good with faces and names. I'm in outside sales; it's a necessary skill for my job. I'm also pretty sure I'd remember an Asian mom and daughter. I mean, really other than my siblings I don't see that many kids ever, it's not like I work at a school. Last time I checked, the bars me and my friends go to on the weekends are pretty kid-free. I'm positive I've never seen Sonja before in my life. So what the hell does it mean, this man in the red suit?

I got home from work tonight about six and turned on MTV2, planning to zone out on videos for the hour or so before *24* started on Fox. A White Stripes' video came on where Jack White was walking around a house in a red suit. This should have made me laugh at the irony, but I freaked out. I dropped my drink and my heart started racing. I don't know what the hell happened to me. I scrambled for the remote and by the time the set got shut off I was sweating. Mr. T stared at me from the kitchen table intently; I could hear Sonja's voice.

"The man in the red suit is looking for you Jake."

It's almost midnight now; the weather channel is on in the background. First snow of the year should come tonight. I take a sip from some Swiss Miss I just made, and look out the window. My reflection stares back at me from the glass.

"The man in the red suit is looking for you Jake."

It's dark and the snow hasn't started yet. It doesn't matter though, I already feel cold.

Parental Guidance Strongly Suggested

Because of my father, I saw my first pair of naked breasts and watched Mohawk Guy die all on the same day. I was eight years old when, on a Tuesday in 1984, everything changed for me. I never saw my father, breasts, or violence the same way again. It was wonderful.

Simply put, my dad loves the movies. Some men love football, others beer, but cinema has always been Don Stednitz's drug of choice. We were one of the first families in my hometown to own a VCR. It was a hulking RCA VHS model that loaded movies through a jack-in-the-box style top-loader. My father achieved a regard usually reserved for the rich families with pools when people came over to watch the miracle of movies at the Stednitz house. This was largely because my dad in Gretna, Nebraska had the only VCR on Earth that came with a "remote control." This was state of the art in 1980.

The remote was enormous by today's standards. It wore Star Wars footie pajamas religiously and looked exactly like me. My earliest memories are not that of my dad teaching me to read little golden books, but of my father teaching me how to stand on a box and load movies into the VCR. I learned that the fat button was Stop and next to it was Play. The neighbors would marvel as I would be handed a movie and then operate the VCR for their viewing pleasure. By the time the FBI warning hit the screen, I would bow to thunderous applause, my dad beaming with pride.

It has always been movies with my father. They're the touchstone of our relationship in many ways. My freshman year of college when my father had a heart attack I remember telling my girlfriend I was so afraid he wouldn't make it because we had agreed to see the new Star Wars movie together. When I first introduced my father to the girl I was going to marry, we all went to see *The Matrix*. The day before I got married my father and I roared through *American Pie 2* with drunken groomsmen in tow. However, of all the films my dad and I have seen together, none stand out more than the one we saw that Tuesday in 1984.

"Do you want to go see *The Terminator* today?"

I looked up from my two dueling He-Man figures in disbelief. My dad had his "going into Omaha" Nebraska Cornhusker ball cap on. He stood in my doorway casually, as if he hadn't asked a life changing question. It was as if he had asked if I wanted a sandwich or if I had remembered to let the dog out. He actually had his car keys in his hand, as if he really intended to go see *The Terminator* with me. To be clear, my disbelief was founded due to the Patsy Act. This insane *Terminator* plan was a clear and decisive act of high treason, a willful and obvious violation to the Patsy Act.

The Patsy Act had gone into effect a few years prior due to *The Raiders of the Lost Ark Debacle*. Patsy Jo, being my mother, had been mortified the last ten minutes of *Raiders*. She watched stunned, as my eyes filled with horror, terror and glee. Nazi's faces were being melted off right in front of me on the screen! This was not the movie she had in mind when she took her six-year-old son to the theater.

Now, in fairness to my mom, my dad had sold the idea of taking me to *Raiders* as, "It's a movie starring Han Solo and it's about him looking for church stuff. It's like a religious, adventure movie."

Once back in the car, free from any melting Nazis, Patsy explained to my father (in PG-13 language) why I was never to be allowed to watch "blood and guts" again. The Patsy Act was written into law without a vote.

So to find us in the same car a few years later, sans Patsy on the way to see *The Terminator* was a momentous occasion. I was in awe of my father. Could my dad be this cool? I was going into the uncharted territory that was a rated R movie, the Patsy Act be damned!

Now for the record, I had no idea what *The Terminator* was about, but what I did know was that it was rated R and it had a really cool poster. I had asked my dad what *The Terminator* was when the whole family had gone to see *Baby: Secret of the Lost Legend* the weekend before. Before my dad was able to answer, my mom reiterated the key statutes of the Patsy Act.

Walking past the ticket guy, I caught my dad looking back at *The Terminator* poster. I stopped and studied the poster for a moment: Arnold in his sunglasses, looking scary and cool at the same time. He was like Han Solo meets The Boogeyman.

I wonder if my dad had concocted his *Terminator* plan that day, seeing me staring up into Arnold's Ray Bans. Had my dad sat at work during his break pondering if I was ready to take down an R? Maybe he realized how much attention was going to my baby brother at the time and knew that seeing a movie with just the two of us would be a big deal to me. I realize chances are good that on that Tuesday he probably just wanted to go see *The Terminator* and didn't want to go by himself, but who can really say?

Regardless of the motivation, the Tuesday trip to see *The Terminator* was clearly a special occasion because my father continued his defiance of all things Patsy. Not only were we seeing a blatantly banned film, but as we passed the turn by K-Mart and kept going straight. I shot my father a look of disbelief.

He smiled, rubbed his beard thoughtfully and asked smiling, "Did we just miss our turn to Cinema Center? Guess we'll have to go to The Twin."

Q-Cinema Twin a.k.a. The Twin was known in my house as "the expensive one". It was the theater that the people who lived in Devonshire went to. The people that lived in Devonshire, which was the subdivision on the other side of the highway, included my dentist and my doctor. The popcorn at The Twin automatically came with butter and the ticket guys wore vests and bow ties. I had gone there once in my life prior to *The Terminator* when my friend Geoff and his family took me there.

The Twin was kind of like a church in my mind. It housed two auditoriums with giant movie screens. They were so big they had to have a slight curve to them and they filled your entire field of vision like a lo-fi version of virtual reality. A tapestry where the paintings were created with light and big enough to take you away, immerse you completely, baptize you in cinema.

As we pulled into The Twin parking lot, I felt the importance of the moment weighing on me. I was about to join the elite club of kids who could see rated R movies. It was the 3rd grade equivalent to losing your virginity.

Keep in mind this was still a couple of years before *Indiana Jones and the Temple of Doom's* famous voodoo-heart-ripping-out-of-the-chest scene that would enrage Patsy and moms like her around the world. These enraged moms would go on to pressure Hollywood to come up with Hollywood's greatest cop out ever: PG-13.

In 1984 we were still in a very black-and-white world. There was only R or PG. In school this meant you either saw movies for MEN (which we clearly thought we were) or movies for BABIES (which we clearly weren't). So to be in the parking lot of the Q-Twin with the intention seeing *The Terminator* was a clear validation of my adulthood. My father was recognizing I was a man now. I half expected him to offer me a beer. My dad had left my baby brother Dustin home with mom and insisted they not get a sitter. This was an outing for The Guys, not for Babies or Girls.

"You ready to go?" my dad asked smiling. I was already running out of the car.

When we got to the ticket counter I began to panic. What if this was all just a joke? But then my father asked for two tickets to see *The Terminator*. I nearly yelped.

"Sir, just so you know, it's rated R due to violence and nudity."

I distinctly remember wishing that Ticket Girl would melt like a Nazi, but then my father said something that I repeated to teachers constantly throughout the rest of my elementary school years.

"That's okay, he's advanced for his age," my dad said pulling my Husker hat down over my eyes. My teeth that would within months be confined by braces stuck out stupidly, an awestruck smile.

Walking into The Twin, my Catholic instincts made me want to dip my hand in holy water and cross. Their posters were all in glass frames, the floor was free of popcorn carnage. The guy tearing our tickets called us "gentlemen." When I asked him where the restroom was he called me "sir." Sir. I had a ticket to an R-rated movie. I wasn't a kid anymore I was now Sir-Damien-the-Advanced-for-His-Age.

So it was with this great welling of pride and budding machismo that I followed my dad down the aisle and we saw *The Terminator*. There were not enough melting Nazi's in the world to match the awe I had for this film. My 8-year-old jaw dropped, only closing to eat the occasional kernel of buttered (for free) popcorn. My mind was officially blown.

Arnold was bigger than life; he looked like He-Man without the page boy hair cut. My former concept of bad guy, Darth Vader was trumped in the first five minutes of the movie. Arnold's robot killer in the opening five minutes punched through Mohawk Guy! He didn't just punch him; he punched all the way *through* him!

Sure, by today's standards one death in the first five minutes by punching is pretty tame, but in 1984 from an 8-year-old point-of-view this was a brave new world. My dad wore a sly grin as I furiously began eating popcorn following the death by punching.

"This guy is a bad guy, huh?" my Dad asked me.

"Worse than Skeletor," I replied, eyes transfixed.

My jaw remained dropped through the car chases, the cool gun with the laser sight (I immediately began taping pen lights to my squirt guns), the scene where Arnold cuts out his own eye, the melee at the police station, the colorful use of the F-word (there are phrases I learned in *Terminator* that I still use on the 405 on a daily basis) and of course, the love scene.

Ah, the love scene…Linda Hamilton. Seeing this scene at eight, I was speechless. Its significance at the time was largely lost on me. It was as if I filed the scene away in my mind realizing it was somehow important. I realized at some future point the information of Linda Hamilton naked may be of some value to me…it was. All through my high school years, Linda Hamilton's breasts were the ones by which all others would be judged.

Yes, *The Terminator* taught me a lot. I learned new phrases, had a whole new threshold for gore, and ultimately a new baseline by which I judged how cool a movie was. I was now a man.

The ride home was near mania. My dad laughed most of the way home, agreeing with me that he also couldn't believe "the good guy" had died and that Arnold could definitely beat up Darth Vader, but that Arnold vs. Godzilla was too close to call.

I started every sentence with something along the lines of, "wasn't it awesome when he…" or "I couldn't believe it when…" I could barely contain myself.

"Did you have fun?" my dad asked smiling.

"It was better than *Star Wars*," this being the greatest compliment I had at my disposal at eight.

My father went on to tell me how his dad had taken him to see Vincent Price in *The House on Haunted Hill* and what a great movie it was. I only remember this because at the time I had no idea what he was talking about or why. I wasn't really interested in talking about anything on the way home that didn't involve cyborg killing machines from the future. I stopped him mid-sentence to get his take on whether he thought Arnold could beat the Huskers. He answered with the "of course not" that I fully expected.

I recapped the entire film for my friends underneath the tornado slide in North Park numerous times throughout the summer. The F-word, which was critical to the story recap, became less and less foreign to my mouth after each retelling. It was clear to my friends I had matured. Until around that September every time I left to do my paper route I would tell my mom in a horrible Arnold impression, "I'll be back."

To which she would reply an increasingly confused, "I know?"

Now don't get me wrong, is *The Terminator* a movie that every 8-year-old should see? No, I agree it is not. Was my dad making a statement to me about my maturity when he took me to see it? No, he probably just wanted to see *The Terminator* and knew my mom wouldn't go with him. However, when people are reminiscing and they ask me to recall my favorite childhood memories, seeing *The Terminator* with my dad is up there on the list. It was the first secret my father and I shared and during a time in my life when a lot of focus was being placed on a baby brother this was one day that stood out as mine.

We all eventually moved on from *The Terminator*. Arnold obviously was back like he promised in *Commando*, *Predator* and *Total Recall*. Linda Hamilton enjoyed success on TV in *Beauty and the Beast*. My mom loved *Beauty and the Beast*. I would feel something like guilt watching Linda Hamilton on the TV with my mom. Every Wednesday I would have to watch Linda running through the TV subways with Ron Perlman's Vincent and the whole time I was watching all I could think was: I've seen her breasts. It was the definition of awkward.

With time even Mohawk Guy recovered from his fatal punching. Though it wasn't until I saw *Aliens* that I learned his name was Bill Paxton. He would become my mom's favorite actor by playing Chet in *Weird Science*. To this day my mom laughs at the thought of Chet getting turned into a pile of crap at the end of the movie. She also refuses to call Bill Paxton anything but Chet.

"*Aliens* had too much blood and guts, plus I hated that Chet died."

"Your dad rented *Predator 2*. It was stupid, plus I hated that Chet died."

"Damien, have you seen *Titanic*? The scientist guy at the beginning is Chet!"

"I just don't believe Chet would ever risk being killed by a tornado for Helen Hunt."

"Have you seen that new show on HBO where Chet has all these wives?"

I'm doubly glad my mom has never seen *The Terminator,* seeing Chet get punched through would simply be too much for her.

I figured a lot out even past Mowhawk Guy's identity as time moved forwarded. I realized that not all R-rated cyborg movies were good (i.e. Van Damme's *Cyborg)* and that not all time travel movies were good (i.e. Van Damme's *Timecop*). I figured out that the F-word probably shouldn't be part of language used at school. I learned a lot, but some things I didn't grasp.

By the time *Terminator 2* came out I was in high school and had long since stopped going to movies with my dad. I was far too cool for that. On the Saturday when he asked me to go with him I remember thinking it was weird that he asked me.

I had already seen it with a bunch of guys from school and declined the offer. He went and saw it by himself at the Cinema Center. When I asked him what he thought of it when he got home he said it wasn't as good as the first one.

Looking back now I realize I didn't return the favor of letting him into my club. It's only looking back now as an adult that I recognize the disappointment on his face. Harry Chapin would have appreciated the irony. Unlike *The Terminator*, we can't go back and change the past. We screw up, time marches on having its way with us, credits roll whether I'm watching them with my dad or not.

Luckily Hollywood always has another sequel ready to give us another crack at a happy ending. *Terminator 3: Rise of the Machines* hit after I graduated college. By this time I had moved to Texas, but was going back to Nebraska for a friend's wedding a couple of weeks after *Terminator 3's* release. I called my dad and we both agreed not to see it until I came home so we could go see it together. I still maintain that the only point of the mid-20's is to repair the mistakes made in your teens.

For the record, *Terminator 3* is a horrible, contrived movie. Arnold phoned this one in more than he did in *Red Heat* or *Raw Deal*. I truly believe for most of the film he's literally just reciting in his head over and over "don't look old, don't look old…" Additionally, the pairing of Claire Danes and Arnold in the same movie works about as well as having Eminem and Dick Cheney do an album together.

The Q-Cinema Twin Theater is still in Omaha, sort of. It wasn't bulldozed, but evolved into something else entirely. Its evolution is similar to that of the villains in *The Terminator*. Arnold was the bad guy in the first one, a T-800 terminator robot. By the sequel there was the T-1000 terminator played by Robert Patrick. The T-1000 was a new and improved terminator, the evolution of cyborg killing machines. The high number of 1000 was used to emphasize how much more dangerous the T-1000 was than Arnold's outdated 800 model.

That's what happened to the Q-Twin Theater, it morphed into something more dangerous with a higher number. It became the Q-Cinema 6 when I hit 5th grade. It graduated to the Q-Cinema 9 when I was in high school; and is now the movie carnival that is the Q-25. The words "cinema" and "theater" have been dropped from the name because the screens at Q-25 are roughly only 10% larger than the screens in most living rooms. Q-25 does boast a full arcade, three different types of nacho cheese, a coffee bar, and nomadic packs of 15- year-olds that attempt to give you involuntary Lasik surgery with their key chain laser pointers. You do get a free cup (think Dixie) of popcorn if you say "Go Huskers" on game days.

The Q-25 and theaters like it all over the country are a pretty close approximation to the theaters I think are in Hell for when Satan wants to force someone to see *Mission Impossible 3* or *Gigli*. I've always thought Satan probably loves J-Lo movies and any sequel that's part 3 or beyond.

My dad and I had a good time at *T3* regardless. We talked during most of the movie, caught up on what was going on in our lives. We discussed being married to headstrong women and my dad asked about when I was going to have a son of my own. It was the first conversation I had with my father as a peer. Once more *Terminator* was the backdrop for a moment of maturity in my life. I noted the irony of having these talks with my father during *T3* because in a lot of ways I felt like a sequel trying to be as good as the first.

We also did some time traveling of our own during the end of the film. My dad laughed remembering seeing the first *Terminator* with me.

"You were so excited; I can't believe you didn't tell your mom. Do you remember how crazy you were after that?"

I laughed and told him I remembered. Did he really think I would ever forget my first R-rated movie? It remains one of my happiest memories of my father. As the credits rolled we left the theater joking and laughing: two men, two peers, two friends.

Felicity Huffman

I watched Felicity Huffman
at the Oscars,
I was rooting for her.
(She should have won, by the way,
no offense Reese, but anyone involved
with *Legally Blonde 2* should be
barred from the Oscars for a
punitive period of like
ten years. Of course, I guess in a year
where *Penguins* beat *Murderball* we
were going for cute and non-threatening
as an Academy over honest and edgy.)
Anyways, I was watching Felicity
when I saw she was married to
William H. Macy. He was the husband
in the movie *Fargo*…you'd know him if
you saw him.

It got me wondering how their
marriage is working out.
I mean, five or six years ago
Willy H was a hot commodity.
He'd been up for the Oscar and
it seemed like every movie made in
1998 had him or Steve Buscemi
in it.

I'm sure at the time Felicity
was happy for Will. Success
for your spouse is a great thing, but
also she's trying to make it in the business
too right?

So here's Will blowing up with fame
and Felicity's got bit parts in
Showtime original movies
that Will's starring in and
directing.

Moreover, I wonder how are they doing now?

Felicity is white-hot with *Housewives*
and the Oscar nod. Her agent has
probably got his phone on vibrate just
so he doesn't have to hear his Black Eyed Peas
ringtone again.

And where's Will in all this?

He's pretty much on the side,
with a smile,
holding a purse.

I saw an interview with Will
and he said he's so proud
of Felicity's success and
I believe him…

it's just…

Jayme got her doctorate last month.
I worked the whole time she went to school,
even caught a few promotions on the way.
I'm a modern, sensitive
21st century digital boy and
I know all about the fish and the bicycle,
but I have to admit

I enjoyed putting my wife through school.

I enjoyed taking care of her
and in spite of all my liberal enlightenment
there was a very *Little House on the Prairie*
satisfaction to winning the bread.

Now I'm proud of her, at least
as proud as Will is of Felicity, maybe more,
but I bet if I ran into Mr. William H. Macy at a bar
and if we had enough beers to
where our insecurities could float
to the top like foam
we'd find we have something in common:

we're both afraid our wives don't need us
as much as they used to.

Maybe Will would put
his hand on my shoulder and express
drunken confusion as to why Felicity stays,
when she's on the rise and
he's just holding steady.
Maybe that's when I'd have
the epiphany,
as bright as my new doctor's smile.

I'd put my arm around Will in reassurance
and I'd let him in on the secret.

"It's love Will, it's always been love."

Jeff Wilson

there was a five year stretch
where Jeff Wilson was my best friend
Han Solo was my hero and all
I really wanted was the Millennium Falcon
for Christmas

Andrew Marvell was right about time
I'm 30 now and I don't even know
where Jeff Wilson is, what he's doing
if he's married or not

I know nothing about him

but there was a time when I was six
that I told him I wished he was my brother
rather than the stupid baby

Jeff's the only person alive that
knows I really broke the snow globe
and that it wasn't Dandy the Dalmatian

I hope he's doing good
if he has a little boy I wish him a friend

as good as his father

Luke Skywalker (is a Boy)

I'm telling Jayme about the Star Wars
X-Wing fighter I got when I was five.
It was awesome.
A classic in orange plastic made by the
fine folks at Kenner.

We were talking about great Christmas presents.
I had just gotten done hearing about her Barbie house
her dad had built that was taller than she was.
She still has it at her mom's house
complete with the tea set in the Barbie kitchen.
I wonder if she ever even played with the damn thing.

So anyways, I'm telling her about my X-wing fighter
that carted my Luke and R2D2 action figures
around and how I got grounded because
I dug a hole in the backyard and filled it with
hose water to simulate the Degobah swamp planet.
(It was 1981 and everything was all about *The
Empire Strikes Back*.)

The hole itself wasn't the groundable offense, but
it didn't help.
The problem was my mom watched
her young son climb up the stairs to the
top of the deck
and then throw his brand new $14.99 toy as hard as he could
off the deck, into a mud puddle
with an anticlimactic splash and the sound of snapping plastic.

For me the crash was perfect.
I ran down the stairs quickly,
Yoda in hand so he could use The Force
to rescue Luke and the ship.

My mom was furious and fast
catching me before I got Yoda to the crash site.
No one could understand I just wanted it to all be like the movie,
even if it did mean the ship snapped off a wing.
I accused my mom of being an agent of Darth Vader as she
drug me screaming up the stairs.
I pretended I was Han Solo captured by the Empire as I spent
the rest of the day in my room, sulking, knowing Luke was
sinking into the murky depths of Degobah.

Jayme processes the story
and begins to rub her belly muttering
"Be a girl…be a girl…be a girl."

Jesus vs. The Snooze

I'd go to church more
if it weren't for the snooze
button that takes up the entire
top of my alarm clock

a large enough button
that even a hung over
half asleep arm can hit it
denying salvation

the devil's not in the details
he's in the snooze
I'm biting that damn apple
nine minutes at a time

Los Angeles to Las Vegas

nothing holds more promise than
the Thursday night drive to Vegas
everyone is a winner
as the car radio plays your theme song

Jayme is sitting out of the passenger window
she's singing along to a Tony Bennet song
that she thinks is a Frank Sinatra song
that she insists on hearing every time
we go to Vegas

we pass through Primm
Jayme cheers something about outlet malls
we're dangerously close now

Eric is laying in back counting hundreds
and telling us again about the deadly
system for craps he's read about online that's
sure to win

Jayme crawls back in but only to
start the song over and then back out the window
her knees stare at me
her hands keeping the beat on the roof of the car

as my friends perform their various
rituals I smile and thoughts of successful
double downs and triumphant all-ins
make my foot hit the gas a little harder

Eric's systems
Jayme's laughs
my daydreams

accelerate on to Vegas

three winners who only have yet to arrive

Las Vegas to Los Angeles

I'm up eight hundred dollars
Jayme's out in the backseat
Eric's driving, he's down a grand
but up a blonde named Shayla
a UCSB sophomore
he ran into as she was coming out
of a Cirque de Soleil show her
eyes still filled with residual wonder
her phone number in his wallet
filling the void nicely where
ten one hundreds sat on Thursday
folded with potential

I'm up eight hundred dollars and
the Sunday morning drive is a desert death march
we have shirts rolled up in each
of the windows weakly providing shade
my head is splitting like
black jack tens

twelve hours earlier
I was up three thousand
Jayme and I bouncing from
room to room like a roulette ball
landing finally in 2342
a room party hosted by
army recruits who somehow
had infiltrated a college women's
basketball team

two thousand dollars turned into five kegs
and countless bottles
strangers turned into friends
I woke up in a bathtub wearing
a basketball jersey

I'm up eight hundred dollars and
we're still three hours from home
Eric is singing to the radio
Jayme is sleeping off the rum she
drank out of a combat boot
in 2342 there's a six-foot-one blonde
with great legs, a better jump shot
and my Pearl Jam t-shirt

I'm up eight hundred dollars
but on the ride back from Vegas
I always end up feeling
like I just broke
even

Moonlight, Sunday Night, I Don't Feel Right

I'm driving fast trying to escape
The moon that's chasing me down
It's a game I've played
Since I was eight

I'm twenty years old now
And there's something missing
In my life

I doubt that it's a cheeseburger
And a pack of Reece's Pieces

But that's all that I have

Items in the Overhead Bin Have Shifted During Flight

leaving California
is ripe with connotations
every trip to the Midwest
holds the potential of permanence
brothers and sisters and friends
are hooks and strong line
the pond is small and I can
be a very big
very exotic fish
a former salt water breather
in fresh waters

yet

every time I swim back
upstream
to Los Angeles
a near instinctual pull
I cannot explain

Night Surf 1

the fray of flight is over
luggage is in the room
wake up calls have been arranged

Jayme and I crash into beach chairs
a different, unfamiliar ocean crashes into rocks
forgotten stars welcome us for the first time in years
Los Angeles smog thousands of miles away

my fingertips find Jayme's
for what seems likes the first time in years
Los Angeles is thousands of miles away

we lost four hours coming here
but gained a lot more

Meaner Geese

they have meaner geese in Puerto Rico
but the bartenders are a lot nicer
not that this mattered much to Jayme
running through the resort screaming
geese in hot pursuit

My New Friend, Benny

"Sir, looking at the bill you can
see I gave you two drinks on the house."

I literally swam up to this bar.

Lifeguards may have to fish Jayme out in an hour.
My tip floats well past forty percent.

My new friend is Benny,
he is all that is right with Puerto Rico

My New Friend, Karlos

"Young lady do you want another drink?
If you do, I will need to use the blender again.
The only way I can use the blender again
is if the rest of this pina colada in it disappears."

Jayme adores the attention.
There is the flourish of inverted blender
and with that her third pina colada finds itself
full again at no charge.

My wife is aglow, with the blender now empty
her new drink can be born.

My new friend is Karlos,
he is all that is right with Puerto Rico

My New Friend, Franco

"I am sorry my friend
we do not have the little umbrellas.
To make up for this let me get you another pina colada.
It tastes like pineapple and love even without an umbrella."

My new friend is Franco,
he is everything that is right with
Puerto Rico.

Pigeon

I'm drunk in a pool
a pool with a bar
failing at trying not be obnoxious
when a pigeon lands at the bar
heading for the peanuts
by Jayme and I

it halts
torn between
its desire for peanuts
and its fear of us

much like I'm silent torn
between my desire to
not look like a drunken ass
and my desire to
try to say something funny

the pigeon goes for the peanuts
I hear my mouth talking yet again

K'roja!

the man at the wheel is José
and he is perhaps the greatest
flashbulb friend
I have ever known

you know these people
you meet them by chance
the one time acquaintance
that burns bright
has tremendous impact
and then is gone

maybe they're next to you on a plane
or perhaps you get stuck in an elevator
or in our case, they are driving you
to a lagoon for a kayaking trip

on the way José explains his friend
owns a bar where they make their own
sangria, sangria known as
k'roja sangria

José then laughs deeply, a laugh
that I'm convinced comes from the
bastard son of Vincent Price and
Speedy Gonzalez

Jayme asks but he refuses to translate
k'roja, but says it means the sangria is good
we've been in the taxi an hour now
a drink sounds well-earned and local

we walk in: a blonde in a bikini and her
husband in a Pearl Jam t-shirt
we scream *American tourists*

brown faces at the bar turn, disinterested
then José enters behind us

there is a verbal explosion
we are now local
the bartender, Jorgé, does not speak English
but Jayme's cough and tears after her first taste
explain universally that k'roja sangria is not for her

pina colada's dance with her the rest of the evening
I, however, find myself seduced by k'roja sangria,
made in the back, poured from a used Hawaiian Punch bottle
Jorgé slaps me on the back approvingly, smiling as I drink

José mentions I'm a poet and the karaoke mic
finds itself in my hand
I do poems about Puerto Rican bartenders
those that understand English smile and applaud
those that don't cheer wildly, just because there's a white kid
on stage talking fast and throwing his arms around

the drinks begat drinks which begat drinks
José is on the phone and I'm vaguely aware of the fact
that there's no way I'm going kayaking this evening
José's sons and son-in-laws arrive with José's daughters
there are numerous introductions

Jorgé is cheering behind the bar and a bucket
a literal bucket of k'roja sangria is being ladled out
Jayme is even having some by this time
at two we find ourselves singing along
to Van Morrison on the jukebox
Spanish and English mashed like mojito sugar and mint
brown-eyed girls singing about themselves

it is our greatest night in Puerto Rico

I live in Los Angeles, a reflecting pool of a city
it has a beautiful image, but no real depth, a city of stars
but no constellations

I'm from the small town Midwest, a place of simplicity, slowness
and relationships strengthened by thousands of winters
but winters that leave you bleak and bland

as I watch the Puerto Rican sunrise
through the bars of a bar's window
I realize I have found something
that I have been looking for

I survey my new friends in various stages of disarray
at various tables
Jayme's asleep on the bar, a party hat from who knows where
lopsided on her head, José's two sons sit silently playing dominoes

I walk out into the moist, sobering dawn
Jorgé and José are smoking on the porch
I join them for a shared cigarette, we smile

we are community

Perfect Light

there's a lagoon in San Juan
at an apex of the Bermuda Triangle
where the water glows when disturbed
bioluminescence
thousands of microscopic
plankton reacting to stimuli

the light they create is
perfect
literally
man-made light is inefficient
it produces heat
energy is wasted

this light is pure light
immaculate
clean

only light

I glow treading water
I am six years old
I am the lightening bug
an angel

The End of America (for JK)

We're sliding down slowly
on the 405.
The white snake slithers
at a snail's pace
past the red snake I'm in.
The 24-pack that was
going to help us celebrate
the weekend is now
buried under hastily
packed luggage.
I dread LAX.
Jayme's curled asleep
riding shotgun.
She's cried out.
My eyes burn,
threatening to betray me.
I see the Getty on the hill
and crack a paradoxical smile.
Your visit last June
we looked at two paintings and
then just hung out in the green space,
catching up, laughing,
feeling young.
We listened to your theory
that the Getty would be the place to go
if zombies took over:
secure,
restaurants with food,
plus a lifetime of art to look at.

As the Getty slips by,
my smile dissolves.
I guess you were always planning for the end.

The phone that delivered the
bad news an hour ago vibrates.
It's Pat.
I let it continue its silent ring.
I'm not ready to talk about it.
I'm sure Pat's calling just to
relay the message that your mom
already gave me
or worse, maybe no one's told
Eric yet.
Voicemail takes away that burden.
Telling Jayme was bad enough.
She still has the picture of you and her
at the Halloween party,
Batgirl & Catwoman,
stuck in the mirror in our bedroom.

The exit to LAX snaps me
from memory.
It is creeping up lackadaisically.
My blinker flashes with best intentions,
but I don't turn the wheel.
I'm not ready for this to be real.

The exit floats by.

I'm now out $800 bucks.
I imagine a couple on stand-by to
Omaha becoming thrilled to find seats.
Jayme will understand, so will Pat and Eric,
I hope your mom does.

Traffic washes us out
to Santa Monica.
The car stops at the shore,
Jayme's awake now,
she's okay with not going.

We're on the same page, always.
I rescue forgotten beers.
Jayme's hard to find in the dark.
I find her near the night surf,
she's absently building a pile of sand.

"You remember sand volleyball?"
she asks, I smile once more.
The Tuesday night regular game
you organized, a weekly reminder
that graduate school wasn't prison and
that we weren't adults yet.

Jayme and I drink and reminisce your finest days.

"This is it isn't it?" Jayme asks.
I finish a beer and nod,
everything will change.

In one night I am made old.
In two nights, friends bury our friend.

Jayme and I grow old
at the end of America,
beyond us is only sea.
There is no America left.

Empty bottles behind us
we join hands and run off
America and into cool waters.
Shoe are ruined,
you would be proud.

We dive into cold uncertainty,
leaving America and youth ashore,
hoping to be reborn.

Wham Me

I read in Entertainment Weekly
the guy who hosted
Press Your Luck
died last month.

He seemed like a good guy,
always optimistic and empathetic.

Do you remember this show?

The lights flashing around the board,
taunting epileptics:

Big Bucks! Big Bucks!
No Whammies!

STOP!

The whole thing a big
bi-polar morality fiesta
set to synthesized beeps.
Greed pushing school teachers
and mechanics toward
big bucks euphoria,
but always in the end
the draw wasn't in the victory.
It was in the defeat,
personified by the anti-Christ
of 80's materialism,
the breakdancing, cartoon devil:

The Whammy.

How many college funds?
How many shiny new Huffy bikes?
How many Betamax VCR's
did The Whammy moonwalk away with?

Contestants left broken
their pastel collars upturned
wishing John Cusak could
hold up a boombox loud enough
to drown out The Whammy's
cruel laughs.

Now there's a famous episode
you can Google,
it's actually a two-parter,
where this crazy ice cream
man named Michael actually
memorized the board's patterns
and beat The Whammy.

Michael the Ice Cream Man
pressed his luck 43 times in a row,
successfully.
He moonwalked away a cult hero,
a game show legend and a hundred
thousand-dollar millionaire.

I saw an interview with him on
the Game Show Network.
He put the money into real estate
and lost it all.
Looks like The Whammy
got him in the end.

So here I am,
stuck,
watching the lights
flash around the board.
The spaces light for
brief strobed seconds:

Big Bucks!
New Baby!
Faithful Dalmatian!
Yellow SUV!

I stand,
sweaty palms over
a buzzer
unable to
STOP
because The Whammy whispering
doubt on my shoulder,
he might be right.

1-UP

I saw the best minds of my
generation unified by Nintendo.

The *Legend of Zelda* had a
gold cartridge.
In a world of dull, gray plastic
it stood alone.
A beacon during our post-*Donkey Kong*,
pre-girls confusion.
Zelda was our first true love.

My life changed that Tuesday at Target.
I hovered around *Zelda's* display case,
a moth, enraptured.

The world changed that day.

For those two weeks,
myself and 10-year-old boys across the
country were Linked to our televisions,
in 8-bit euphoria,
to save Princess Zelda.

She was our moon landing.
She was our British Invasion.
She was our Elvis.

Thumbs blistered with effort.
A's and B's pressed with determination
and desperation.
Princess Zelda was the burden thrust upon our
pre-pubescent shoulders.
We had been called.
We had been chosen.
We would rescue Princess Zelda.

Sometimes, especially on long flights,
if I'm seated next to a guy roughly my age
or worse if there's an extra guy because I'm
sitting middle, I like to mention *The Legend of Zelda*.
It's that touchstone for late twenty-something males.
Without fail, there is a moment where my
fellow flyers' eyes show flecks of that *Zelda* gold.

I do this because it spares me the usual macho
verbal swordsmanship where we politely
compare: cars
              colleges
              kids
              careers.

This fake, forced, competitive, small talk bullshit that happens on
every flight because clubbing each other to
determine dominance went out about 2,000 years ago.

By mentioning *The Legend of Zelda*, we avoid all this.

Instead
we spend a flight
talking about those 14 golden days,
in the summer of 1988,
when we were brothers.
When Princess Zelda
needed us.

It's funny, because looking back
I don't think the princess was the
one who was really saved.

Weight

The neurons in my brain feel
your absence.
In the space between them
there is a lack of the neurotransmitter
serotonin.
There is a lack of the neurotransmitter
dopamine.
This, in turn, generates a somatic response.
I become inert,
tear ducts fill, empty.
A weight settles in place.

I could take something for this,
a selective serotonin reuptake inhibitor
or a serotonin norepinephrine reuptake inhibitor.
Neurotransmitters would replenish and
become more abundant in the synapse.
The space between would fill,
chemistry would fool my mind.

But I don't.
This sadness has a weight
that I want to hold,
that I want to have
for a time.
I need to experience this.

I need to feel the weight of this
because it means that we mattered.
It means that you mattered.
This weight ties me to my memory of you.
It matters and it means
that we were happy
for a time.

4 0 5

I hate you

I hate you so damn much

I hate everything that is you
I hate the false promise that is
your car pool lane
I hate the Tupac album next to me
I'm forced to endure at full blast
because of you
I hate the stick figure family
in front of me I'm memorizing
because of you
I hate the constant political
bumper sticker debate I sit through
because of your clogged arteries
I hate the bad influence you've
infected your brothers the 5 and the 210 with
you are like everything I hate about New York
laid down in a concentrated strip in the
middle of this angelic city I love
I hate you for being the only part
of this city that makes me long for
the Midwest once more and
your beautiful distant cousin
I-80 with her ease of movement
her constant accommodation
I dream of the flying car
to free myself of your restrictions
when we have flying cars
the Capitol records building will be even
more reminiscent of *The Jetson's*
flying cars darting through the airspace
Blade Runner set to the California sun
once the cars fly you will be forgotten 405

except I will remember you
and I will take my antique ground-based car
and drive to you in your obsoleteness
and I will spend my remaining days
jack-hammering you into oblivion
I will feel like the East Germans tearing down the wall
I will laugh as I break you into pebbles
I will smear your dust on my face
and feel like Mel Gibson in *Braveheart*

I will destroy you
you asphalt pariah
you nemesis

you freeway that is neither

Juicy Couture

Me: It's a sweat suit that costs $250 dollars
You: Eva Longoria wears them
Me: It's a sweat suit that costs $250 dollars
You: Lindsey Lohan has eight pairs
Me: It's a sweat suit that costs $250 dollars
You: Gwen Stefani wore them all the time on her last tour
Me: It's a sweat suit that costs $250 dollars
You: They make my ass look fantastic!

The dressing room door swings open…
you're right
my hand unconsciously reaches for my wallet
there are some arguments I just can't win

Batwoman

So Batwoman is gay.

I don't mean that like I used
to say that Aquaman is gay,
which was just my junior high way of
saying that being able to talk to fish
isn't that great of a superpower.
When I say Batwoman is gay
I mean that Batwoman is attracted
to other women,
not other Batwomen,
just other women in general.

This apparently is a big deal:

Bill O'Riley talked about it in his No Spin Zone.
Nancy Grace talked to two different experts about it.
Anderson made it part of his 360,
but the real kicker:

there was a protest today outside
the comic book shop I go to.

(It's right by a church.)

I was mortified as I went in to get
my Saturday dose of
Green Arrow, *The Walking Dead*,
The Goon and *Spider-Man*.

There were all these pissed off soccer moms
blocking the door
yelling at me like I was some
15-year-old trying to get an abortion
rather than just some 30-year-old

trying to get the only literary fix
my ADD brain can handle these days.

I had fifteen women with signs yelling,
I mean passionately yelling,
telling me that Batwoman is a bad role
model for their kids.

Okay, now I'm not going to point out the obvious
facts that there are people dying overseas and that
we're all going to be washed away in thirty years
when the ice caps melt and that Batwoman's
sexuality should be pretty damn low on people's list of
"Shit That Passionately Pisses Me Off."

What I am going to point out is that
every single time the Incredible Hulk gets upset
he smashes everything and everyone around him.
Superman, Wolverine, and Batman
can't seem to resolve any conflict without punching
someone in the face.
For some reason Wonder Woman can only fight
crime if she's half-naked.

Yet no one worries about
these super individuals' effect on the children.
No, they're fine,
because even if he has pummeled fourteen or fifteen bad guys
to death and maybe a few buildings in the process
the Hulk goes home to She-Hulk.

No, who we're worried about is: Batwoman.

Look, I'm not trying to oversimplify this.
I get that there's a lot of personal, spiritual,
religious, and emotional pieces that go into this
issue.

But look gang, I've never been to Gotham City,
but I've seen pictures and I think it's a lot
like Los Angeles:
there are people with nowhere to live,
kids getting beat by parents that should love them
and families on a near daily basis getting letters
that their son or daughter has died fighting in some desert.
If Batwoman at the end of the day
has someone,
anyone,
man or woman,
that can hold her,
love her,
tell her that it's all going to be okay,
that it's all worth fighting for,
that we're worth fighting for…

I'm okay with that.

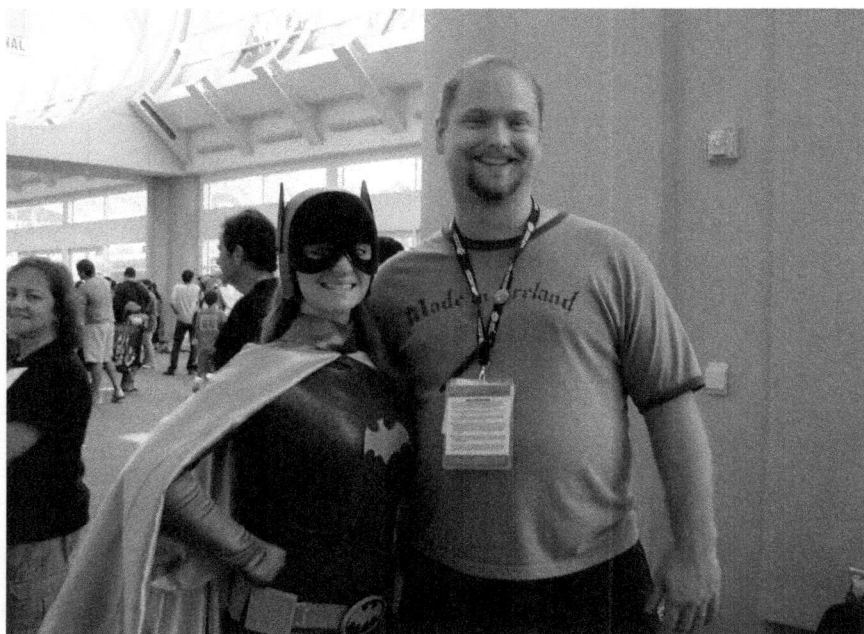

My (X-files) American Dream

so I had this dream where
I was David Duchovony
well, not really David Duchovony
I was Fox Mulder, the character
he played on *X-Files*
and I'm in this bar
and since I'm Fox
I'm looking for The Truth
when I see this metal
door labeled The Truth
which I'm thrilled by
because my objective is pretty
much done and I can soon enjoy a beer
so I pull on the door
and Donald Rumsfeld puts
a hand on my shoulder and says
you can't open that
and I see with his other hand
he's making an iron fist
and then Jack Nicholson
yells that I can't handle what's
behind the door
I pull on the door anyway but it's locked
Anderson Cooper comes running to me
with a crowbar, he manages to throw
it to me before Bill O'Riley trips him
and they begin to fight on the floor
rolling and biting like a pack of
Wolves Blitzers
I put the crowbar into the seam and
try to pry it open, but I can't get it
Jesus is standing right there and
I ask him to help and he sighs
and tells me

"My son, I'm tired of always being used
as leverage to achieve a goal."

I look for assistance from anyone else
but the only other people around are
Dan Rather and Katie Couric
sitting at a table looking very serious
Dan keeps saying to her over and over

"Don't question and keep them afraid,
we must keep them afraid."

since I'm an average American
at this point I say the hell with it
and go to watch *American Idol* at
the bar
I ask the bartender for a beer, something
dark
he gives me a pint and I take a well deserved
swig, only to spit it out
"This is oil!"
I yell, irate and confused
the bartender smiles and tells me
"That's where the money is kid
speaking of which you have to
pay for that whether you drink it
or not"
I give him a five and he tells me
the only currency they take is
dead soldiers
I can pay him 1 American or
10 Iraqis
I tell him the only soldiers I know
are my little brother and some
kids my brother used to play
soccer with when he was nine
the bartender says, "sucks to be you"

and Private Joey Milner
the best 9-year-old soccer goalie
my hometown ever saw
dies in Fulijah

this isn't right
I need to tell someone
someone has got to know about this
this isn't right

voices behind me hiss
"No, this isn't right, it's The Right!"
I turn and
Karl Rove and Darth Vader
suckerpunch
me in the gut
as I'm doubled over Karl and Darth whisper
to me that

I need to work on my Patriot Act
I need to get a bumper sticker
I need to vote for an Idol
I need to go to church
I need to buy a Humvee and fill it up for $118
I need to stop causing problems
I need to stop trying to open that door
I need to play Xbox, listen to my iPod
and stay afraid
eyes fixed to the TV
watching yellow to orange to red
afraid
afraid
afraid

Opening Band at the Roxy, Saturday Night

they're not bad, the opening band from Victorville
they're thrilled to be playing the Roxy
playing Hollywood, a tough town to break into

I'm thrilled to be at the Roxy, to be in Hollywood
thrilled to be at the bar before the opening band starts

the bartender has a tattoo and a great smile
during my obligatory small talk
she tells me John Lennon
used to get drunk at the
Roxy on brandy alexanders
I try to order one
follow John's lead

they don't make them anymore
I end up feeling like a tourist for asking

I try to order a mojito
trying to find left over residual coolness
from my trip to Puerto Rico
they don't make them, no mint leaves
the bartender gives me a beer I've never
heard of,
"It's cool, you'll like it. Everyone here is drinking it"

I look around and see young guys from the indie record labels
drinking beers with a label on the bottle matching my own
feeling Hollywood I walk to the front
the young no-bodies from Victorville
are about to play to a crowd of no-bodies

everyone doing their best to be a star

Headliner at the Roxy, Saturday Night

the guitar solo is loud and everlasting
Jayme's eyes are lit up, this was the song I played
on cassette, on the way to work the summer of sophomore year

this was the guy Jayme and I drove to Texas to see as juniors

this is the song I sang karaoke to at that bar in Burbank
when we first came to LA

this is the guy we both agreed was great
his album was the original motion picture soundtrack
to the movie that was our college years
this is the guitar solo we've
crashed to, cried to, cleaned to, cooked to

this guitar solo is a touchstone to that first date at that bar
the initial small talk we made, this song played in the background

my ears ring on the way home
this ringing has been constant since
I was fourteen
fifteen years of guitar solos
absorbed by my body

the ring on my finger
constant since I was
twenty-four

love

ringing
everlasting

The Day I Decided to Apply Myself in College

freshman year was spent
trying to be cool
on rollerblades
at the end of beer bongs
and ultimately doing the obligatory
finding of myself
only to find myself
not really all that cool
but ultimately in love

now love takes money
because without TGIFriday's
how is a young college girl to know
that it's a date

this financial obligation of love
is how I found myself
at Biotech Services to sell plasma
$30 your first visit
$40 if you come back in the same week
it seemed like a good plan
$70 a week plus
they showed movies while
plasma was pumped and peddled

so one day in January
I found myself
in the aforementioned love
hooked to a machine
watching Kevin Bacon ruin
any credibility HG Wells's
The Invisible Man ever may have had

everyone else in the room was a junkie

I had donated blood before,
but this was different
one, there was no cookie
two, it lacked that do-gooder feeling
(I just felt like a sell out)
three, after they take what they want
they pump the rest back into you
(you feel it in the roof of your mouth)

donating blood you're The Buffalo and
the Red Cross they're the Indian tribe
they use everything and you are exalted
selling plasma you're The Rhino
the lab are the poachers that sheer your horn
and leave the rest

I lied there, looking around at
human debris hooked to cutting edge technology

this wasn't where I wanted to be

the next day I got a part-time job
to fund my quest of love over Caesar salads
and buffalo wings
I studied more and went to class
I found a path

sometimes I'd see Biotech ads in the school paper
and my veins would cringe, my plasma would hide
I had moved on, and wouldn't go back

I know still I sold a little piece of myself there

To The Daughter I Didn't Have

I dreamt about you a lot
over the last five months
your name was Harper
and you had gold curly hair
and your mothers eyes
you laughed a lot and loved
Hello Kitty and sometimes
pulled our real cat's tail
but we allowed it because he's
declawed and your laugh made
it all worth it
your mom loved to dress you
in hats and dresses and bows
and there was a stack of comic books
that I had prepared for you in case you
were a boy that got forgotten under
dolls, and flowers, and a tidal wave of pink
(your mom and I are educated enough to know
we shouldn't gender code but we did anyway)
and Harper it was going to be great
a pink nursery with frills and ribbons
your mom and I had cleaned out Baby's R Us
of both their sugar
and their spice
I was ready for you in these dreams
to protect you from the world
my little girl
to save you from all the stupid boys
them of puppy dog tail origins
I would spin you on the merry-go-round
faster and faster, the wind filled with laughter
you convinced no one in the world
could be stronger or faster than
your dad

Harper, you were vanished in a sonic boom
we saw that you were not the person we thought you were
on that grainy, lo-res screen
my dreams had misled me
your mom giggled and somewhere a snake bought a snail a beer
the comic book stack grows daily now
I find myself wondering where I can buy a baseball glove
and Spider-Man has regulated Hello Kitty to the garage
where she waits for you, forgotten, next to unopened bows &
ribbons

autumn has come and in spring a blue hurricane will hit
your mom and I enjoy the falling leaves, the calm before the storm

I pushed a merry-go-round today, just once
while walking the dog, watched it spin
I heard a dream girl laugh in the wind
Harper I truly hope to see you again

My Reserve Has Not Been Met

my 17-year-old sister emailed me a .jpeg today
her in her new blue, butterfly shaped sunglasses
she saw a model wearing them in a magazine
typed "blue butterfly sunglasses" into Ebay
and bought a pair for $6.99 from a woman in Arkansas

a generation ago, she would have gone to the mall in Omaha
which probably wouldn't have carried them
so her and her friends would have probably made the weekend
trip to Kansas City, to the giant mall

they'd of had fun during the 4 hour drive
stopping at gas stations to buy sunflower seeds
trying to get carloads of boys to honk at them
having those conversations you have during the
final hours of a roadtrip
who's hotter Shaggy or Fred
laughter would have filtered down the highway at 55mph
maybe she would have found the sunglasses in Kansas City
maybe not, by the tired Sunday ride home it wouldn't really matter

there was a book by Dylan Thomas I was always looking for in
college
a screenplay he had written called *Rebecca's Daughters*
I never found it through my numerous quests through used
bookstores
however, at one used bookstore I met the cat that ran security
he chased my untied shoelace religiously as I poured through
disorganized stacks
the cat's name was Mookie, the owners a couple named Kevin and
Steve
due to Mookie's fascination with my shoes we had a good laugh
that turned into coffees and great discussions about books and old
records

Mookie is probably still in the window, waiting for shoes
Kevin and Steve I hope still run the store without a register

at another store, I failed to find *Rebecca's Daughters*
but I found a set of green eyes on the other side of a bookshelf
that I fell in love with for a time
the eyes owner was a girl named Marie
a smile, led to coffees, which led to dinner
which led to 18 months that ultimately didn't work out
but it could have

I bought *Rebecca's Daughters* on Ebay, like my sister got her
sunglasses
I got it for $12.99 plus $2.99 shipping from a seller in London
I sent him an email profusely thanking him, explaining how
long and fruitless my search for the book had been
I got a form email back saying, "Please leave positive feedback"

no
no, I'm not going to leave positive feedback
look the internet…
the internet is a net and there's a whole generation caught in it

I can't leave positive feedback, because my reserve is not met
what I want, is to want

I want to wait, anticipate

I don't want it right now, with a Buy-It-Now click
I want to sit at an empty table and hope you show
and watch the street corner hoping you're coming around it

what I want is the only thing not for sale on Ebay
my reserve has not been met

the internet is a net
choking the life out of my generation

Details

I'm good at talking to people
I remember little things
I know when to keep talking, when to turn back
I smile and remember birthdays, kids' names, vacation spots
the details that breed trust
I coach people how to talk to doctors for a living
I remember the little things
I'm good at talking to people

the old woman in the waiting room forgets her husband's name
she has sliced tennis balls on her walker, her hands shake
her glazed eyes turn to me, turn back to her husband
Lauren and I smile politely and then continue
going over the pending detail
I coach Lauren how to talk to doctors for a living
I remember little things
the old woman in the waiting room forgets

the little girl is glowing, blonde curls
I watch the old woman's eyes follow the young light
she whispers "that girl makes me want for to turn back..."
her hand reaches weakly, brushes gold hair for a moment, a smile
then Alzheimer's erases the details, her light dims again
her husband coaxes her hand to her lap; this is the life he's living
I remember little things
the little girl is glowing, blonde curls

what good am I talking to people
I want words for the old woman and her husband
words to turn it all back for them
words that say something that delivers a smile
words that remind them of the details of their past
but her light is going dim, erasing, he holds her hand, living
the little girl is glowing, blonde curls
the old woman in the waiting room forgets
and I remember these little things

Ruining Los Angeles

I didn't see you and I almost hit you
that's my fault, but you didn't need
to roll down your window and call
me a stupid fucking bitch
you don't know me
you don't know my situation
and if I'm being honest
and at the risk of sounding like a 4th grader
you really hurt my feelings

the 405 sucks and none of us want to be on it
we're all just trying to get home
Los Angeles is tough enough as it is
we all have cars so we can seal ourselves
up in our own individuality
we don't know our neighbors
and none of us are from here
we're all just trying to make it
we're all just trying to make this work
and for you to take the trouble to
stop talking on your cellphone
honk to get my attention and then
roll down your window just to call me a bitch
it just adds to the overall frustration and
negative bullshit and further solidifies
the fear we all have that maybe everything
everyone not from here says about us is true
that we all are a bunch of shallow, hateful
non-caring, just in for ourselves pricks and
that when it all falls into the water no one is
going to be that bad off because it's all about
the money and ourselves and
where we're going and not about
the woman in the other car and what her story
is and that sucks because dammit we have so much potential

we're all just trying to make it
and we could all be in this together we could all
work to help each other out and it wouldn't take a lot
just maybe letting the other person in for a change
or maybe just borrowing a cup of sugar from your neighbor
just so you can introduce yourself or finding out the
dry cleaning lady's name and maybe bringing her a
cold bottle of water one day because it's like
100 degrees in there and maybe when someone
makes an honest mistake you for once don't scream obscenities
at them and then have that horrible awkward ten minutes
where we both have to sit next to each other in traffic
because we're both stuck next to each other
trying to get home
and when I see you crying…

I mean when you see me crying…

I mean when I see you crying
I realize that when I write about this
I need to be honest
and I can't have me be you
and you be me

my name is Damien Stednitz
I am ruining Los Angeles
I am sorry for that
we should all be in this together

Author's Note

There's a ton of people that I would like to thank for their support and inspiration in putting this book together. First and foremost, a huge debt of gratitude is owed to my wonderful wife Jayme. Thanks babe, without your support none of this writing stuff could happen.

Another heartfelt thanks goes out to all my friends whether you be a Dragon, a Weasel, part of the Strategic crew, part of the Forest crew, or one of the poor bastards from Lubbock. You've all had an influence and some of you pop up in these pages.

I'd also like to thank all the amazing writers I've met over the last few years: Andrew Mealy and the regulars at Barnes & Noble who have been so supportive, everyone at the Cobalt, the Pasadena library gang, as well as James Levin and the whole Pricilla's group. You have all had an impact on me with your work and I consider you all friends.

A special thanks to Rick Lupert, Terry McCarty, Kevin Patrick Sullivan and Don Campbell. Thanks guys for letting me feature at your respective venues, it meant a lot.

Lastly I'd like to thank you for picking up a copy of the book, I hope you liked it.

About the Author

Damien Stednitz's work has been published in: *Astropoetica, Contemporary Rhyme, Poetry Superhighway, True Poet Magazine, The San Gabriel Valley Quarterly, Flintlock, Falling Star Magazine* and *Speechless Magazine*.

He has done several featured poetry readings throughout the southern California area. He is 34 and lives in Los Angeles with his wife, Jayme and their two children. Damien loves Pearl Jam, updating his Facebook status, reading comic books and the fact that you read this bio.

Also by Damien Stednitz

www.ingramcontent.com/pod-product-compliance
Lightning Source LLC
Chambersburg PA
CBHW060422050426
42449CB00009B/2082